AF480603

Getting Ready for™ a TORNADO

A Calm and Helpful Tornado Safety Book for Kids

This book belongs to:

____

Written by Dr. Fei Zheng-Ward

Illustrated by Moch. Fajar Shobaru

Identifiers: ISBN 979-8-89318-155-5 (eBook)
ISBN 979-8-89318-156-2 (paperback)
ISBN 979-8-89318-157-9 (hardcover)

Sometimes the weather can change.

Lightning flashes, thunder booms, and rain falls.

One kind of storm is called a tornado.
A tornado is a strong, spinning wind.
Spin your finger like a tornado!

A tornado looks like an upside-down cone.
It reaches from the clouds to the ground.
Some tornadoes are wide like a funnel.

Some are thin like a rope.
Which one looks like a rope to you?

Tornadoes can move fast, and they can be loud.

They may change direction or spin in one place.
Having a plan helps us stay safe.
Safety Plan

Tornadoes are also called twisters.

They are two different names for the same storm.

Tornadoes happen most often in spring and early summer.

But they can happen at any time.

Learning about tornadoes helps
us stay safe and prepared.

Weather scientists study the weather, watch the sky, and help keep us safe.

BOOM
BANG
CRACK
SNAP

Sometimes a tornado gives us clues that it may be coming.

Let's learn what to look for.

Big storms with lots of thunder and lightning.

A very dark sky that can sometimes look greenish.

A loud rumble, like a train or whistle.

CHOO–
CHOOO!

Tornado winds can be very strong.

Strong winds can move trees, branches, and other loose things.

A tornado forms when warm air and cool air meet.

The air then spins faster and faster and round and round like in a spinning dance.

Most tornadoes do not hurt people because we have safety plans and know what to do.

Many tornadoes are small and last only a short time.

Weather scientists send warnings before a tornado.

A warning means it's time to find shelter and stay safe.

Don't worry. Grown-ups will help you know what to do.

When there is a tornado warning, go inside a building and stay there.

You can go to
a basement
or an
underground
shelter.

If there is no basement,
go to a small room away from windows.
Get under strong furniture and curl up like a roly-poly (or pill bug).
Protect your head and neck.
Stay away from windows and things that could fall.

You are so brave!

A safety kit can help.

Let's name what's inside!
CRACKERS
SNACK
SNACK
SNACK
Flashlight and batteries
Water
Snacks
Blanket
Stuffed animal
Who's your safety buddy?
☐ My grown-up
☐ My blanket
☐ My stuffed animal
☐ Other ______________________________

When you know what to do,
you can feel calm and brave.

Preparing for a tornado helps you
stay safe and ready.

You've got this!

Did your child enjoy this book?
If so, I would love to hear about it!

www.amazon.com/gp/product-review/B0GS7KDSRZ

For other book titles, please visit:

www.fzwbooks.com

Connect with the Author

email: books@fzwbooks.com
facebook/instagram: @FZWbooks

Books by the author

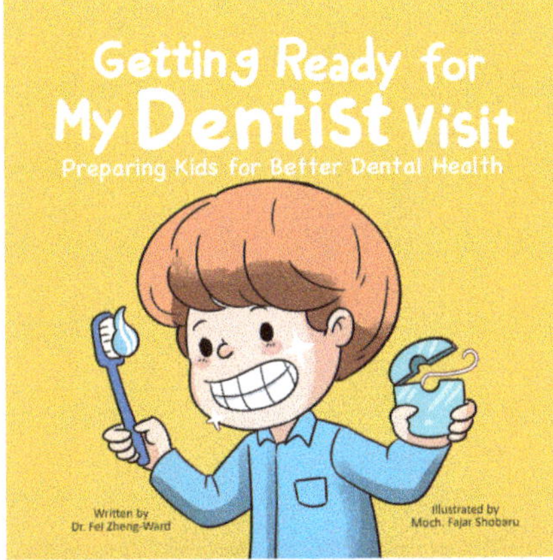

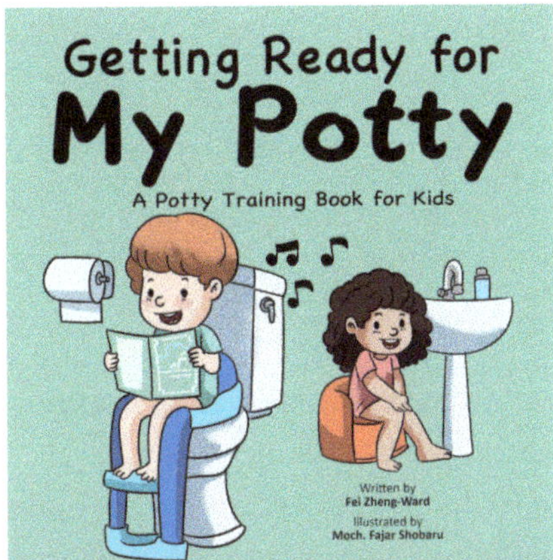

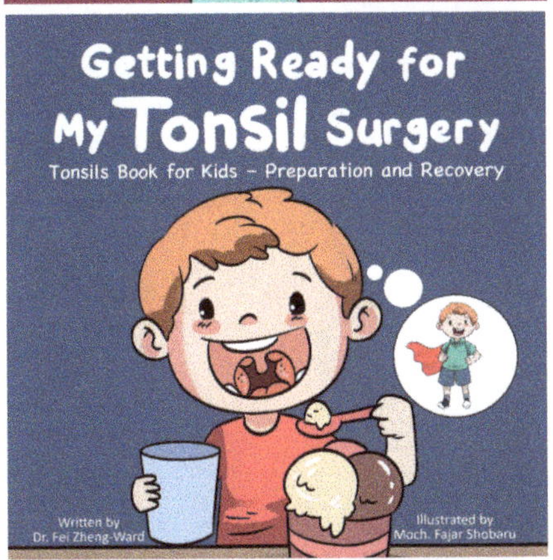

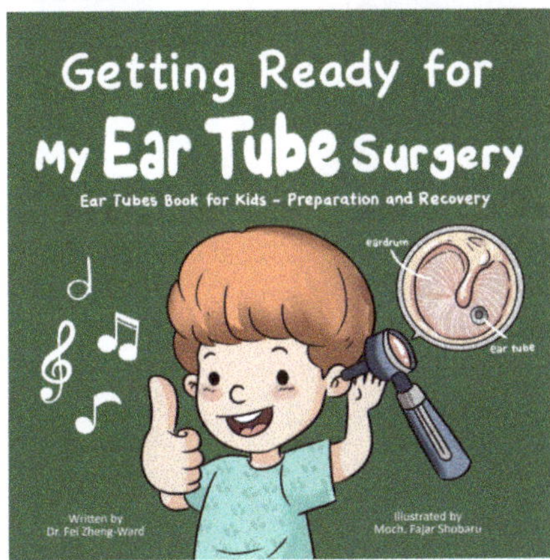

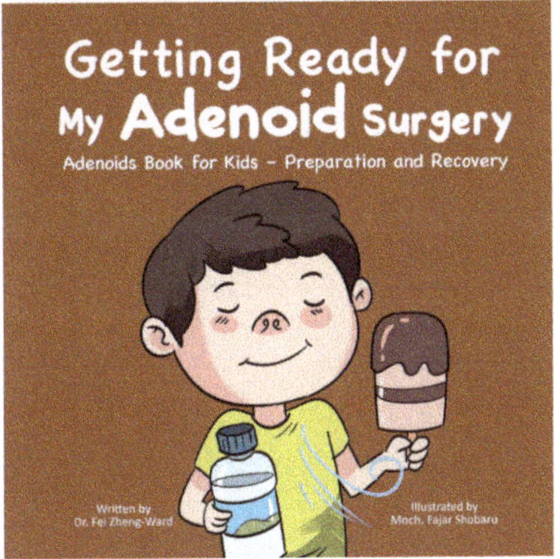

Forever and Always
By Your Side
Fei Zheng-Ward
Nabila Amanda

Beautifully, Uniquely You
Geoffrey Ward
& Fei Zheng-Ward
Nabila Amanda

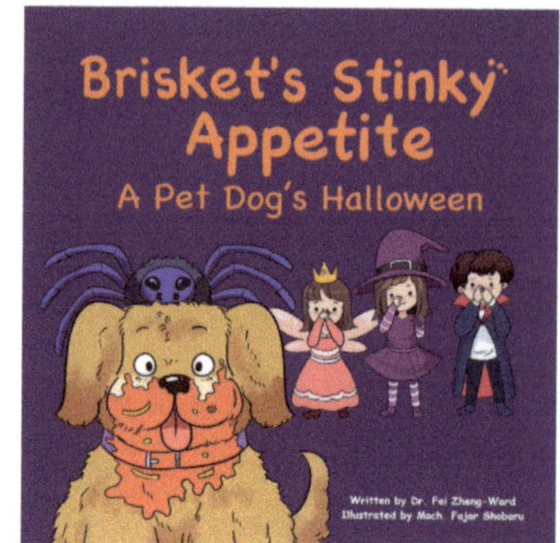
Brisket's Stinky Appetite
A Pet Dog's Halloween
Written by Dr. Fei Zheng-Ward
Illustrated by Moch. Fajar Shobaru

MEATBALL'S ADVENTUROUS APPETITE
A PET CAT'S HALLOWEEN
WRITTEN BY
DR. FEI ZHENG-WARD
ILLUSTRATED BY
ROKA STUDIO

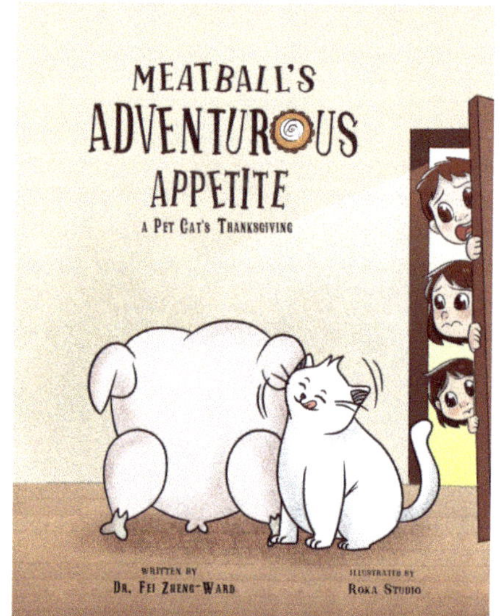
MEATBALL'S ADVENTUROUS APPETITE
A PET CAT'S THANKSGIVING
WRITTEN BY
DR. FEI ZHENG-WARD
ILLUSTRATED BY
ROKA STUDIO

MEATBALL'S ADVENTUROUS APPETITE
A PET CAT'S CHRISTMAS EVE
WRITTEN BY
DR. FEI ZHENG-WARD
ILLUSTRATED BY
ROKA STUDIO

VICTORIA SAVES THE DAY
A BOOK-READING GIRL OUTSMARTS A WITCH
Story by
Geoffrey Ward & Fei Zheng-Ward
Illustrated by
Nabila Amanda

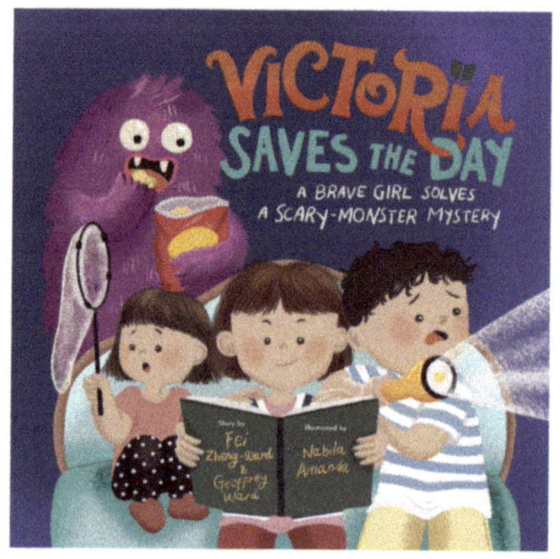
VICTORIA SAVES THE DAY
A BRAVE GIRL SOLVES A SCARY-MONSTER MYSTERY
Story by
Fei Zheng-Ward & Geoffrey Ward
Illustrated by
Nabila Amanda

VICTORIA SAVES THE DAY
A CLEVER GIRL PLAYS TOOTH FAIRY
Story by
Geoffrey Ward & Fei Zheng-Ward
Illustrated by
Nabila Amanda

www.ingramcontent.com/pod-product-compliance
Lightning Source LLC
Chambersburg PA
CBHW041816130726
48010CB00004BA/184

9798893181579